THE
BLUE BALLOON

JOURNEY *through* GRIEF

Sally Mathews

Sifting and shaping
Kathryn Schifferdecker

Cover art and watercolors
Janice McMurray

Pen and ink drawings
Carole Jo Dennis

Book design
Elise Nicol

Lewisburg, PA

Grateful acknowledgement is made to reprint the following:

"Acquainted With the Night" from THE POETRY OF ROBERT FROST edited by Edward Connery Lathem. Copyright © 1956 by Robert Frost. Copyright © 1928 © 1969 by Henry Holt and Co., Inc. Reprinted by permission of Henry Holt and Co., Inc.

"Poem" from THE DREAM KEEPER AND OTHER POEMS by Langston Hughes. Copyright © 1932 by Alfred A. Knopf, Inc., and renewed 1960 by Langston Hughes. Reprinted by permission of the publisher.

"Lord of the Dance" by Sydney Carter. Copyright © 1963 by Stainer & Bell Ltd. All rights reserved. Used by permission of Hope Publishing Co., Carol Stream, IL 60188

"On Children," "On Friendship," and "On Death" from THE PROPHET by Kahlil Gibran. Copyright © 1923 by Kahlil Gibran and renewed 1951 by Administrators C T A of Kahlil Gibran Estate and Mary G. Gibran. Reprinted by permission of Alfred A. Knopf, Inc.

Scripture verses are quoted from the King James Version of THE HOLY BIBLE.

Library of Congress Control Number: 2013920061
ISBN: 978-1493554539

Printed in the United States of America

It was always for

CAROLE JO

THE
BLUE BALLOON

JOURNEY *through* GRIEF

PROLOGUE

At first it was just raw pain,
and writing was something I could do with that pain
in the dark night hours.
I'd walk the floor,
crying,
stifling the moans,
rocking and holding
myself,
then put some words on paper.
My daughter found the beginnings of the journal and said,

"You should write, Mom, but don't write about Marc."

I prowled libraries, looking for a book about my experience.

I wanted to be with another woman who had
lost a son, walk with her in the solitude, let her
explain it to me, help me make sense of it.

I never found the book.

My son died tragically.

After my son was killed, life and death were more closely
interwoven. Sweet coincidences filled me with hope and wonder,
assuring me that in our deepest pain there are blessings.

I needed to find words for this.

Sixteen years have passed since it happened. Nothing, it seems, has changed.

I am still myself.

We've painted the house a couple times, and now I'm sixty-one years old,
no longer forty-five. The azalea bushes are much larger, even with all the pruning,
and several of the laurel have died. In the midst of so much life, flowering
and green, life was taken. And in the midst of loss we found new life.

Losing and finding, breathtaking mystery.

My son's bedroom is now my study. Today I will peel the old wallpaper off
the walls. We were changed once, and we still struggle with the change.

Slowly,
    imperceptibly,
        regular pruning continues to shape us.

It's 1:05 in the morning, one month from the day Marc was killed.

There have been moments of joy, a realization of love from so many, and there have been moments of grief.

I want to remember it all, the wonder and the pain. How can I feel pain adequate to the brute destruction of my son's young body?

I can't, but neither can I bear what I am feeling.

If only there were some way to tell Marc: I don't like the way this turned out. I see you growing tall and striving to understand, to be. How could anyone destroy that?

I hate it. I'm sorry.

Marc, I am so sorry! Oh, God, I'm sorry!

Why do I keep saying that? I didn't do it. I didn't cause the accident. But the words keep coming:

"Marc, I'm sorry! I'm so sorry this happened. I cannot accept it."

If I write down some memories of Marc, maybe I can keep him alive and part of my life. I can remember how hard he was trying to be gentle. He had grown silent and gruff in the last few years, and he was struggling to change that. At last, he was saying,

"Thanks, Mom, for dinner." When he went out the door, he would say,

"So long."

I'll try to keep true all the grease and dirt.
I will write down that he was sweet and sometimes smiled,
that he was good with young children.
He was starting to be a young man.

I want to remember how it was, that he was alive, bursting with life.
He filled our lives, too.

August 9, 1981, 8:30 a.m.

A few hours of sleep and now the sun is bright. From my deck I greet another day with new possibilities and new life.

The terrible sobs are of another time, last night, not now. I'm learning to welcome the tears. Perhaps little by little, they're washing my heart and bones clean.

But I won't forget.

I've learned that I cannot lie
under the waves of grief
for too long at a time.

They ebb and flow.

I celebrate anguish.
I celebrate peace.

The sun is radiant on the green
leaves. The diffusion of light
through more distant trees
fills me with a sense of spirit.

Red birds
blue birds
brown birds
squirrels
butterflies
marigolds
and green everywhere.

On this new morning, I believe in life!

I will remember this, too.

Sunday evening, August 9, 1981

This was a good day.
We went to three different places
looking for a puppy to adopt.

Energy and buoyancy,
an interest in living,
these carried us through the day
clear into evening.

Such a day, alive all day,
has been rare.

A letter came today from Ed and Audree Bauman. Ed is the Senior Minister at our church, but they're summering at their cottage in Maine. They speak of their own son's fascination with motorcycles, the constant anxiety. Ed says,

"And in our Christian faith, we know that all is well with your Marc. It is the separation that is so hard." Their letter reminds me of a story that is dear to me.

Marc was just a little boy, four or five years old, and Carole Jo would have been six. She loved Sunday school, but her brother did not. Marc often begged to sit with me in church rather than go to his class.

One Sunday during the service Dr. Bauman introduced a new idea, a "Passing of the Peace" that involved hugging our neighbors.

Ooph! How embarrassing!

I hated the idea! Reluctantly, I hugged one or two people, surprised that it felt so good. I was more surprised to see Marc running up the steps to Dr. Bauman who, with a laugh and swooping black robes, leaned over to hug him. When Marc came back to the pew, I grinned at him quizzically.

"Well, everybody was hugging everybody all over the church. Dr. Bauman was standing there all by himself. Nobody was hugging him, so I decided to do it!"

It's a puzzle to me, why there's such grief and pain when a loved one dies. I accept the possibility that Marc has gone to an infinitely more beautiful and peaceful place than we have known, a place where he can learn and grow, surrounded by love.

Why can't I rejoice?
Why can't I celebrate the change?

My love for Marc fell short. So much love was never expressed. The opportunity is gone.

John and I are doing well. At least by all outward appearances, we seem to be doing just fine. I don't understand how or why.

We must be very strong.

Thursday after work, Carole Jo came here to do her laundry. While I slept for two hours, she went to the grocery store and fixed supper, our old standby—tuna casserole. Carole said,

"I'm afraid you're not eating right."

"So what's wrong with tomato sandwiches 37 nights in a row?"

Marc, you know I was opposed to your having a motorcycle. I did everything
I could to stop it. But you sounded so earnest that day on the phone.

"Mom, I don't want to die. I'll be careful."

After months of arguing I finally reasoned that you were your own
person. You had a right to become yourself, even if it included something
I dreaded. You had wanted a motorcycle for years, so I told your dad,

"Do what you like. Help Marc with the loan. I won't oppose you on this."

Marc, you were sure you could meet any crisis.
I feared larger, terrible dangers.
I'm ashamed that my fears were real.

You said,

"If that's what you think, that's the way it will be."

Oh, God!
Did my thoughts contribute to what happened?
I am sick with knowing that I was right.
Somehow, forgive me!

I am remembering a time when all the colors were clear and brilliant. We played in cold water, blue sky and green woods, visiting my brother at his lake cottage. My children's hair shone white and gold in the sun.

Now is a hard time. One golden head has been oiled with muck. Bodies have been ravaged and lost, both my brother's and my son's.

There remains only one way to survive such loss: to love.

My friend, Linda, has died of cancer at the age of 49. She wanted so much to live, and she fought to live. I cannot look directly at her dying. I cannot acknowledge the heartache of her parents; I cannot imagine Paul's loneliness. I don't understand.

What's it about, this living and dying?

A strong cord holds me to a sense of God's presence. I want to believe there is a meaning, a purpose. I will seek to know God, to understand, to love. There's no other reason to live.

How can I endure this pain?
How does a human being survive the wounds?

A friend said recently,

"We can be well in the places where we admit God." How can I open to this pain enough to admit God?

April 17, 1982

Linda and her parents are often on my mind. Whatever I'm doing, in some part of my mind I am with them.

Linda's battle with cancer was heroic, but I couldn't understand her fighting courage. She didn't want to die at age 49.

I would be pleasantly satisfied to be dying!

Carole says to me,

"I am not ready for you to die."

Oh, let me hear that, deep in my heart.
I will be there for Carole.
Surely, I can love that much.

Marc died on Thursday, July 9, 1981. He was riding his motorcycle to the doctor's office to check for a strep infection.

It was an accident. A woman pulled out of an apartment parking lot and did not pause at the stop sign long enough to perceive the oncoming traffic. A police report stated that Marc "laid down" his bike in an effort to avoid collision with her station wagon. A friend told me his skid marks lingered on the road for days.

Nancy, a friend of Marc's, worked at the hospital where Marc was rushed, though she was not on duty at the time. Nancy told me later that the hospital records showed massive injuries: broken hip bones, a crushed pelvic bone, crushed organs. What could have caused such extensive damage?

My guess is that Marc threw the motorcycle out from under himself. The station wagon drove over the top of him and his bike. He was rushed to the hospital and lived for two more hours.

When John and I arrived at the hospital, we entered through its main doors, then wandered down long corridors. Finally we came to the emergency room area, but the two large doors in front of us were locked. Through the glass I could see people sitting in a large room. I knew that was where we needed to be, but we could not find our way through. I started to pull on the doors and knock on the glass, feeling panic rise. A nurse noticed us and asked if we needed help.

"We've been called to the hospital. Our son has been in an accident, but we can't find our way to the emergency room."

"What's your name?"

"Mathews."

"I'll take you there."

She led us through a maze of corridors to an interior station of the emergency ward and into a small conference room.

The attending surgeon entered the room, pulled up a chair, and started relating medical information about Marc to us. I was too agitated to follow what he was saying, so finally I interrupted him.

"Is Marc alive?" The surgeon looked at me carefully.

"No."

John began to whimper, sobs shaking his body, while silent tears ran down my cheeks.

The surgeon continued to describe the physical details in a reasonable voice. Someone brought Carole to the room. I interrupted the surgeon to say to her,

"Marc is dead."

Teeth bared, Carole threw back her head and released an animal wail of grief. The surgeon left the room.

What came next? I remember sitting in another room with police officers. Confusion, this one coming in, that one going out, different ones talking to us. What were they saying? One policeman told us that his colleague had witnessed the accident. He wanted us to know that Marc was in no way at fault, his driving was perfectly correct. I remember the feeling of horror.

"Why are you telling me this? What does it matter now?"

Someone asked us to identify the body, and my immediate reaction was

"No!"

John's expression seemed to say,

"You know this is part of it. This has to be done."

The nurse, ushering us down the hall, asked if one of us might faint.

"No, no one will faint," I answered.

Marc was lying flat on his back on a narrow wheeling bed in a small room. A coarse green sheet was covering him, with an iron brace of some sort fastened at his chin, so his face was all we could see. He looked peaceful. I remember thinking,

"Marc is not here. This is Marc's body, but he's not here. Thank God, Grammy doesn't have to know about this. Oh! Perhaps Grammy does know!"

A sense came to me that others were gathered in the room with us, my mom, my dad, my brothers. How many others? Maybe Marc, too, was there with us, but not in his body.

There was nothing to do,
nothing to be done, really,
except to walk around the
quiet . . . no, not quiet.

Perfectly still.

There has been nothing on earth
quite so still as our son lying,
dead,
under a green sheet
on a long narrow wheeling cart.

There was nothing to do but walk out of the room.

On the day Marc died . . .

We had set up in an antiques show at the Laurel shopping center. It was a wretched day with humidity steaming off the pavement. The heat made a miserable task of carrying many loads from our car into the mall.

John and I had taken care to eat a hearty lunch, and the mall was comfortably air-conditioned, so it seemed strange when I began to feel sick.

It was not just sickness, but a feeling of terrible disorder. I asked John to get me something to eat.

"Is it really as bad as all that?"

"Yes. I feel like I'm going to smash headfirst onto the floor."

I found myself staring hypnotically at the floor. A whirlpool seemed ready to spin me down and throw me against the hardness of that floor. I sat down on a chair and tried to hold on to the whirling world.

John came back, after what seemed an eternity, with a salad. I wolfed it down, but it didn't help.

A while later, Carole Jo and her friend, Tina, came to our booth. Carole was to be the maid of honor at Tina's wedding, and they'd come to the mall to be fitted for their dresses in a bridal shop. They invited me to come with them to eat. I hesitated, then agreed, hoping that eating again would help me feel better.

The kiosk had many types of food, but I've forgotten what I bought. Soon after we sat down at a table, the mall music stopped. Someone announced over the loudspeaker,

"Your attention please. Will Mr. or Mrs. Mathews please report to the manager's office? Attention please! Mr. or Mrs. Mathews, please report to the manager's office."

I stood up to leave and Carole implored,

"Mom, you haven't eaten anything. Eat your food first."

"That's okay. I don't want it anyway. Really, I'm not hungry."

I started to wander, disoriented, when Carole spoke from behind me and touched my arm.

"Mother, come back this way. It's over here."

She walked with me to the escalator and we went gliding down together.

Again, the voice over the loudspeaker,

"Your attention please. Mr. or Mrs. Mathews, please come to the manager's office."

I looked at Carole and grinned half-heartedly,

"All right. All right. I'm coming."

Back at our display, we all looked at each other.

"You stay here and I'll go."

"No, I'll go."

Carole decided for us.

"You both stay here. I'll find out what this is about."

She came back soon.

"There was a message to call David Walden, so I called, and he said the police have been looking everywhere for you. They want you to go immediately to Southeast Hospital. Marc has been in an accident."

Carole began to cry. I put my arms around her.

"Carole, don't cry. It'll be all right. Marc has done this before. He'll be all right."
Her body shook with sobs.

John started toward the doors. I stopped to tell someone,

"We're leaving. Our son has been in an accident," and went running, flying, to catch
up with John. Just as he pushed open the heavy glass door, he seemed to remember me.
He studied my face intently for just a second, as if to say,

"Are you okay? Can you move as fast as this requires?"

Then, without a word spoken, we were hurrying to the car in the relentless heat.

John drove faster than I've ever known him to go, leaning forward at the wheel.

I don't remember getting from Laurel and around the city to the hospital. I do remember that the drive was one loud cry of silent prayer, prayed over and over,

"God, whatever has happened to Marc, be with him.
Whatever Marc must do now, God, give him the strength.
Oh God, I pray that you would give Marc the strength to do what he must do.
Let him know that we love him.
Oh God, let Marc know he is loved."

March 19, 1984

I still pray that prayer today:

Wherever Marc is,
whatever he is doing, God,
let him know that he is loved.

Whatever is happening,
give Marc the courage
to do what he must do.

Dear God, be with Marc.

March 21, 1984

John tells me he had a surrealistic dream about
    Marc, but he doesn't tell me the dream.

"Sunday afternoon is bad dream time," he says.

Freezing rain delayed the schools for two hours today, so John went back to bed and I putzed around in comfortable leisure. I'm starting to get a feel for being healthy again.

So often I have felt like a piece of brilliant glass, shattered. Light dances through the sharp, bright pieces, but they are all broken. I cannot bring the pieces together.

Even if I could, what shape would they take? I have felt so meaningless and frivolous.

Indeed, who am I?

Of what good in the world?

Yet today, the broken shards are lying on a closet floor somewhere.

A measure of peace enfolds me. It seems that I will find meaningful things to do and the means to do them.

I can be an independent person again and perhaps share the good things of life with John. That would be so lovely, a dream come true.

I am thinking tonight of a Robert Frost poem:

> I have been one acquainted
> with the night.
> I have outwalked the furthest city light.

Marc was killed in a brutal accident. That is a fact.

There is no way to change the reality of that fact. It intrudes upon my consciousness in every activity, while making the bed, driving the car, listening to music.

Marc was killed in a brutal accident. It was a tragic mess of human error that caused unbearable pain. Lovely things have happened since that accident. Perhaps if I write them down, the lovely things will acquire a natural weight. Some may be only wishful musings, some not.

I walked tonight in our neighborhood while light rain misted my hair and street lights shone on the wet sidewalk. I am trying to understand these events in our lives.

Tomorrow I will begin to write them down: the blue sky, the mockingbirds, barking dogs, footsteps in the night, Carole Jo's dream.

Tomorrow, I will begin.

Last Sunday Dr. Bauman talked about baptism and the need to renew our baptisms. He talked about the life-giving symbolism of water, whether from the kitchen sink, the ocean, or the rain.

On Wednesday I went to the cemetery to feel the rain on my head, to renew my baptism. As I parked, the rain fell in torrents.

Before I got to Marc's gravesite, however, the dark sky had disappeared. Large white clouds scudded across a sky of infinite blue, and I cried out with joy.

"I am alive!"

"I am in harmony with this living universe and I am glad! At last, I am glad."

When I started my car, I stared at the blue sky through wipers still whipping across the windshield, proof of how suddenly the miracle of blue had come.

That blue sky last week has set me thinking. Marc loved the color blue. We painted his bedroom in a shiny blue enamel to match the sailors in the wallpaper. I remember sitting on the edge of his bed, studying the paint job, when Marc said,

"Mom, tell me again how the sailor boys march right off the wallpaper and around the room. How does that work?"

I had said the paint color was perfect, that it brought the sailor boys right out into the room. I was talking about a good paint selection and Marc saw sailor boys magically on parade.

When Marc was small, I bought a used bike for three dollars, then spent fourteen dollars on spray paint to make a red bike blue.

The second-hand motorcycle was blue, as was Marc's car.

He wears a blue shirt in his high school graduation picture, and the shirt I embroidered for him was blue denim.

Blue was Marc's color.

John's folks went back to Texas about a week after the funeral, and we were alone in the house.

One afternoon I went out on the deck to read the mail. I sat rocking in the redwood chair, rustling the papers, when I noticed a red bird flying in close from my left.

I stopped rocking and held perfectly still as the cardinal landed on the railing, just two or three feet from where I was sitting.

He seemed at ease with my presence, preening himself, rather self-important, unconcerned.

After what seemed a long time, he hopped over to the picnic table and pecked around, flew under the table and pecked about even more.

As I watched the bird, I found myself thinking,

"Is this from Marc? Is he sending me a message? Has he guided this bird to me?"

Finally, the cardinal flew away.

I related the incident to John in a light-hearted way. He must have thought about it, because that evening he said,

"About your bird. That wouldn't have been Marc. He would have sent a mockingbird."

A day or two later John came in the front door, saying,

"Guess what? When I was sweeping the front porch, a mockingbird came pecking around on the bricks near me."

"While you were swishing a broom around?"

"Yes, he got right in there with me, sweeping."

I laughed,

"That must be Marc saying, 'Well, hey! If it's a mockingbird you want, here's your mockingbird!'"

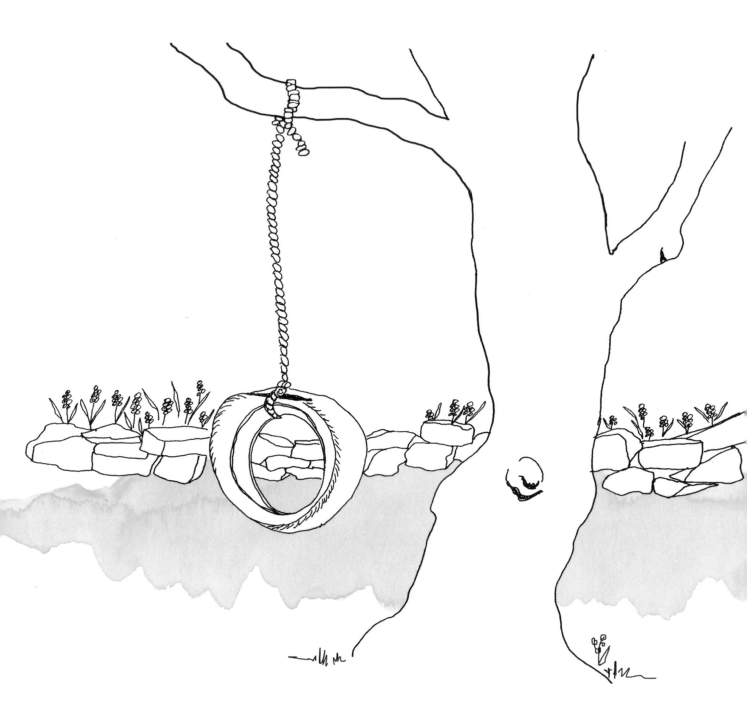

Mockingbirds entered our lives several times after Marc's death. A friend, Marilyn McDonald, had come to our house to discuss plans for a memorial service. For some reason John started telling mockingbird stories from Marc's childhood.

Marc was five or six when the first incident happened. He and Lisa Hill were climbing in the apple tree outside the kitchen window of the Hills' house when Lori, Lisa's mother, overheard their conversation.

Marc was describing a secret club to Lisa, a club he was organizing.

"You can be a member of my club, but you have to take your clothes off."

"Well, I won't do that!"

"I don't care. I can get Carole. She'll do it!"

Lori called me a day or two later and told me what she'd heard. I shared the story with John, who discussed it with Marc.

"How did you know about that?" Marc asked. John told him,

"Well, there's a bird that's helping me, a very special mockingbird. He has a black spot on the side of his head just over his beak. He's the only mockingbird I know with this black spot. He's keeping an eye out for you, Marc, and every once in a while, when he thinks you might be getting yourself in trouble, he lets me know about it.

Now, of course, birds don't go around talking in front of everybody; he only talks to me when nobody is around."

Another time, in the spring, John was out on our roof fixing something, while Marc and his friend, Vaughn, were in the back yard.

With no one in sight, Marc and Vaughn crouched behind a tree and lit matches. John observed all this from his vantage point behind the chimney.

Later he discussed it with Marc, who was concerned with one question,

"How did you find out?"

"The mockingbird told me."

Years later, shortly before he was killed, Marc recalled these stories. He chuckled as he told us,

"For years I studied the birds, looking for the one with a black spot near its beak."

Today I want to write about Carole's dream.

In the early hours of the morning a month after Marc died, I wasn't able to sleep. Grief had me stalking the house, prowling for release.

I'd tried to write, but the pain was too violent within me, so the pen was tossed aside. I opened the double doors onto the deck and stepped into the night.

The trees, the sky, the night, all gathered around me, holding me safe and alone with my grief.

Through my crying I gradually became aware that the neighborhood dogs were barking. With my head thrown back, joining in their wailing, I suddenly became aware of the sky.

Directly overhead a strange thing was happening. I bent forward into sobbing, then stopped, looked back at the sky, silenced, wondering.

A small area, about the size of our dining room, filled with a soft light, darkened, filled again with light. It was not like lightning, but a luminosity that would come to the area, then fade away—a pulsing of light through the darker gray. Weeping gave way to watching, until the light didn't come anymore.

Exhausted, I went inside, locked the doors, and looked at the clock. After 4:30. I prayed that sleep would come for a few hours.

Carole called in the morning.

"Mom, I had a dream last night. Usually I can't remember dreams, but this one was so vivid!

"Dad and I were painting the house. Dad was up on a ladder in the back yard. We needed more paint, so I ran around to the front of the house to get some.

Just as I reached the brick steps, I saw Marc coming toward me. He kind of sauntered, you know, the way he walked, but there was glowing light around him! He said,

'Hi!'

'Marc! What are you doing here?'

'I wanted to let you know I'm okay.'

'Did it hurt?'

'For a little while. I was riding down the street on my motorcycle when I heard a very loud noise. Then I was floating down the river on a log. The log started to roll, and I felt a tight squeezing. That was all.'

'We love you, Marc.'

'I know that.'

'We miss you.'

'I know. I wanted to tell you what happened
and that I'm okay.' He started to walk away,
but with a grin he looked back and added,

'I'm having a good time!'

Mom, I immediately jumped
up and looked at the clock.
It was so real, as though
it had happened right
there in the room!"

"How did he look?"

"He looked wonderful!
He looked just like Marc."

"What was he wearing?"

"What he always wore, jeans and a t-shirt. The only thing was his hair, you know, how his hair always was, blond, but it seemed strange, full of light."

"You said you looked at the clock. What time was it?"

"4:38."

Just about the time I was out on the deck with the sky lighting up and all the dogs in the neighborhood barking.

One night, about six weeks after Marc died, I had fallen asleep and slept for a few hours when I awoke, suddenly alert.

A loud noise smashed into my head, a noise something like a sledge hammer striking an anvil. It hurt my ears, yet somehow it was inside my head, not out in the room.

My shoulders hunched into my neck with the sound, flinching with the blow. Then a buzz like an electric current zipped through one ear and out the other.

I curled up tight, shocked by these sensations, then listened to footsteps crossing the living room.

"There's a burglar in the house!"

But wait.

The footsteps were familiar,
their rhythm, their weight.
I had heard them thousands of times.

They were Marc's footsteps.
They were real.

My mind raced back and forth between fear of someone in the house and the sure knowing that Marc was walking around the living room.

The footsteps came through the hall and stopped at our bedroom door. I knew Marc was standing there in the doorway, looking at us lying in bed.

I no longer felt fear of a burglar, just fear. I did not then, and do not now, understand my fear.

I knew it was Marc.

I could not open my eyes. Squeezing myself shut tighter and tighter, curled into a ball, I prayed, then spoke to Marc, really shouting inside myself,

"I release you, Marc!
I release you because I love you!
I do not keep you, Marc.
I do not hold you.
Go to God, dear Marc, go to God.
Goodbye, goodbye, Marc!
I love you!"

The footsteps turned away. I heard the basement door open, the banister squawked as it always had when Marc yanked on it. Footsteps disappeared down the stairs.

Sam and Bear were barking hysterically, throwing themselves against the closed door of the room next to ours. Their commotion woke John who sat up, put on his shoes, and took the dogs outside.

I lay curled in the covers, unable to move or speak. John brought Sam and Bear back in, shut them in the little room, and came back to bed.

We both went to sleep.

The next morning I looked all around the house. There were no signs anywhere of an intruder having been there. I told John what I had experienced.

"Why didn't you tell me last night?"

"I just couldn't! But you heard the dogs raising that ruckus! When the footsteps came near our bedroom, Sam and Bear went wild, barking! Something had them riled."

I realized then, Sam and Bear wouldn't recognize Marc's footsteps. How could they know he belonged here?

We had adopted the dogs four weeks after Marc was killed.

April 21, 1984

I'm remembering a little more about that time in the hospital.

When the surgeon answered my question and we understood
clearly that Marc was dead, John and I cried.

Then there was no more crying. A few tears at the memorial
service, then long, long days of a parched dryness.

My heart was broken, but there were no tears.

A cocoon, a numbness, enfolded me.

Time stood still or whirled around me, and it was all the same.

I felt very quiet and very still for a long, long time.

As we were leaving the hospital that Thursday night, we met our neighbors, David and Willa, coming to meet us. We were not close friends, but on that day they were uncannily important to us.

The police had been knocking on our neighbors' doors, trying to find us. David remembered John's chance remark about an antiques show at the Laurel Mall. David made the phone call that located us there.

So strange!

Everything was so ordinary. On the hospital sidewalk in the early evening we greeted our neighbors in a long, silent hug.

We walked to our car in the parking lot. Everything looked the same, yet nothing was the same at all.

Our world had collided with something enormous.

My heart was an unfelt, unseen wound pouring blood all over my soul, and my whole body felt sticky with the blood.

We got in our car and drove home.

John, Carole Jo and I were home from the hospital, home in a silent house that said,

"Marc will not come home again."

Marc's room was the usual clutter of his stuff all over the floor. The three of us moved in slow motion to clear the floor, put away the chaos.

For good measure, I took down the girlie calendar from the wall, folded it, and laid it on a shelf in the closet.

Several months later I tried to sort his clothes, to make decisions. I buried my face in a shirt, trying to recover—something. This is a difficult task, I told myself, but just do it.

In one sense it's easy. Fold the clothes and pack them in a couple boxes. My sister, Bev, with her eight sons can use the shirts and sweaters, a suede jacket from the Acme Iron Works, the denim shirt I embroidered.

That embroidery work took hours, and Marc looked handsome in the shirt. The elaborate star across the back pointed up his shoulders, strong and sure on his slim body. I will keep the denim shirt. No, put it in the box. Gathering the clothes was hard.

Marc's accident occurred on a Thursday night. I remember that I called my sister, Beverly, in Iowa. John called his parents in Texas.

I don't think I called Marilyn that evening. I remember picking up the clothes Marc had tossed down the basement steps from the shower.

I held his clothes and treasured the smell, sweat, dirt and dampness.

We made our phone calls. I'd been out of sorts with my sister and had not talked with her much in the year since our mother died.

It took several calls to get the message to Bev.

"Sally, is there anything I can do?"

"I would like you to come."

In his death Marc gave my sister back to me.

During the week of Marc's death our neighbors gathered about us, a supporting family. Mrs. DeLoatch from the corner came down to express condolences, but she began weeping, hugging John out on the brick walk.

Confused, Carole turned to me,

"Why do they come to us, crying?"

I was grateful. I had not known my neighbors would care.

A woman from down the hill brought her children, two boys and a girl. I didn't know the children, but they told me that Marc was their friend. At first I didn't understand what they were saying.

"You knew Marc?"

"Yes. We liked Marc a lot."

"Marc would fix our bikes and give us rides on his motorcycle."

Hungry, I searched their faces,

"Marc did that? Marc gave you rides on his motorcycle? He had time for you?"

"Lots of time. We liked Marc."

I began to cry.

One of the boys put his arms around me, and I could feel my sobs shaking his body.

They brought me a beautiful gift: the picture of my son, almost 19, disappearing down the hill and around the corner on his motorcycle, stopping to play with the neighbor kids.

I had known about Marc smoking pot, but I hadn't known about this.

May 8, 1984

Several lifetimes were packed into those days between Marc's death and the memorial service.

I remember, at some point, answering the door and finding a tall black man standing there. He introduced himself and explained that he was Anthony's father.

Delighted that he had come, I told him Anthony was the first friend Marc had made on his own, when they both started kindergarten.

That first week of school Marc had told me with some awe,

"Mom, I have a friend. He sits with me on the bus."

This seemed wonderful in itself, but pretty soon it became even more wonderful, a person with a name, Anthony.

One afternoon while Marc was taking a nap, I heard a knock at the door. There stood a little boy with brown eyes and brown skin.

"Is Marc here?"

"Yes, but he's asleep now." Then something clicked into place.

"Are you Anthony?"

"Yes."

"Marc will be very happy that you came by. I'll tell him when he wakes up."

Nothing in Marc's description had suggested an African-American child. He hadn't noticed. I had to smile.

Surely the children will lead us.

Years later, when Marc was in high school, Anthony came into our conversation. Marc was grumbling about not having friends in the neighborhood, and I asked him about Anthony.

"Oh, Mom, we don't have anything in common. He's interested in such weird stuff."

"What kind of weird stuff?"

"Things like plays and musicals!"

Weird stuff? John and I were working double-time at my junior high school, preparing a production of the musical, "Oliver!" I ruefully repeated our conversation in the faculty lunch room. The vice principal chuckled,

"Of course, somewhere there's a parent saying to his son, 'Why don't you quit fooling around with all this music and acting nonsense and do something useful, like working on cars!'"

Weird stuff. Plays and musicals and cars and parents and kids and sometimes friends. . .

And now, twelve, thirteen years after the kindergarten friendship, I stood in my living room talking with Anthony's father. How gracious, his kindness in coming by. How grateful I am for all of it.

My friend, Delores, taught me to love the sour taste of wild raspberries with vanilla ice cream.

The day after Marc died, she came to be with me and brought some raspberries that she had picked in a park near her home.

I had just scooped the purplish-red berries onto a bowl of vanilla ice cream and sat down at the dining room table, when my neighbor arrived with her Baptist minister.

I was feeling bombarded by the good intentions of others and had no patience for uninvited ministers come to comfort me.

I ignored the company and dug into the berries.

My mother-in-law came into the dining room, hoping to coax me into better manners. I bent with more resolve over the bowl of berries, my back to all of them in the living room.

The minister talked with my family for a few minutes. I knew they were watching me, but I was determined to keep this time for myself.

The minister came into the dining room. I did not look up. He moved around the table to where I couldn't ignore him.

"I know what you're going through."

Baloney!

How does he know what I'm going through? It must have been a huge helping of raspberries. I hit them harder than ever.

"I've struggled with this kind of loss. My nineteen-year-old son died in Vietnam."

I put the spoon down.

I've forgotten most of what he said.

I know he talked about walking on the beach late at night, kneeling and wrestling in the sand with his pain, aware of the ocean waves and of God's presence.

Then his words brought me to bright awareness.

"This is a clean wound. It will heal. Let nothing get in to infect the wound. It will heal."

A clean wound.

I needed to hear those words. There would be no lawsuits, no blame or accusations, nothing to infect the wound.

After the minister and my neighbor left, I dumped the melted mess down the kitchen sink and fixed a fresh bowl.

I haven't had that treat again, but the image stays with me: ice cream with raspberries and a clean wound.

We knew we wanted a closed coffin for the memorial service. The corpse at a funeral had always seemed to me a strange thing, there on display, seemingly nothing to do with life or death.

Yet, we needed to see Marc's body once more in order to absorb an incomprehensible fact: The son we loved no longer lived in the body we knew.

We planned time at the funeral home for family and close friends to view the body.

I remember standing near the coffin. The hair didn't look right, too slicked down, no life of its own, not like Marc's hair at all. Bev said,

"We could comb it, rearrange it."

"No, let's not mess with it. It doesn't matter."

Funny, they charged us $25 for that hairdo. I should not have let them shave the fuzz over Marc's lip. He must have been trying to grow that mustache for quite a while, and I had it swiped off with one thoughtless yes.

I stood there looking at a lifeless form, familiar and yet strange, not anyone I knew. I didn't touch him.

"You told me you wouldn't do this, Marc. Before you bought the motorcycle, you said you would be careful. You said you wanted to live."

My thoughts wandered back to Marc's early childhood. He was always full of so much energy and excitement! He lost patience over most forms of affection at a very young age, though. No use for hugs and kisses.

One day when he was about four I was holding him on my lap and he was wriggling away. As I let him go, I said,

"Marc, everyone needs loving. Everyone needs love to be a healthy, strong person."

I forgot that conversation until another day when Marc pulled away from a hug, saying,

"Mom, explain that to me again, how you have to have kisses to grow." My little boy.

So now I sat on the edge of a couch in a funeral parlor. No one else was in the room. It occurred to me that I needed to say something, so across the empty room, I said,

"Goodbye, Marc."

Then I sat waiting for the rest of my life.

March 11, 1985

Matt, Mike, David, Steve, Vaughn

Marc's friends came to the funeral home
that Sunday evening, but they did not view the body.

They helped me to know: Marc is loved.

Poem

I loved my friend.
He went away from me.
There's nothing more to say.
The poem ends,
Soft as it began–
I loved my friend.

Langston Hughes

The time with the open coffin seemed to be over. All of us were sitting in other rooms or wandering in the hall. The funeral director decided to close the coffin for the last time.

We followed him, but I stopped in the middle of the room, a good distance from the coffin. I would not get any closer to that lifeless form. It bore little resemblance to a son who had promised me he wanted to live.

The others stopped with me: John, Carole Jo and Jimmy, John's brother, John's parents, my sister, Beverly, and her daughter, Patti.

My mother-in-law's hands were on my back, nudging me forward, but I stood firm with unspoken muttering:

> "Don't be pushing me and showing me how to act!
> I've said goodbye and now it's over."

With each gentle prodding, I became more resolute. Our little group stood there in raucous silence.

Meanwhile, the funeral director was getting flustered. The coffin would not close. He kept lifting the lid and bringing it down, bending over to secure the lock.

It would not work.

Jimmy, John's brother, went striding across the room. Now there were two men, lifting and closing, straightening the white satin, examining the catch, puzzled.

Finally I walked over to them, and John came with me. I patted Marc on the shoulder, while John smoothed his jacket. I had to smile.

Even in death, Marc was calling the shots.

The lid
was brought down
and the lock
slid into place.

John was an agnostic when we married, and he continued to regard church as unnecessary. Soon the children felt they didn't have to go. In fact, none of us went very often during those years when I was teaching public school music. There was never enough time or energy.

One Easter Sunday when Marc was about eight, my family agreed to attend church with me. Marc was disgruntled about going and fooled around getting dressed.

I rushed everyone out to the car, but on the way I discovered that Marc was wearing a shirt with a hole under the arm. A ragamuffin for Easter Sunday at Foundry Church.

Oh well, the main thing was to get there!

The children went to a Sunday school class, while John and I walked into the balcony of the sanctuary. A rush of delight caught me by surprise.

Balloons!

Red, yellow, green, blue balloons! Balloons everywhere! Balloons tied to the podium and lectern, balloons floating high into the dome of the sanctuary.

The azaleas, Easter lilies, brass choir and timpani seemed merely a backdrop for the celebration of balloons.

Near the end of the service children came in from the Sunday school classes carrying huge bouquets of balloons. From the balcony I watched with alarm as Marc walked down to the front with his own enormous bouquet.

"Oh, no! That kid has on a ragged shirt! Don't lift your arm, Marc!"

I began to enjoy what was happening. Marc was in the main aisle on the right, just below our seats in the balcony, a little boy in short pants and a torn shirt, gravely, patiently, working one balloon loose at a time, passing them down the pews, row after row.

Finally, every person in the congregation had a balloon to carry out into the Easter world.

With my ragamuffin son as the giver of balloons, it truly seemed to be my church, my special celebration of Easter, my balloons. What a personal, preposterous, joyful Easter!

On another Easter Sunday, Marc asked me,

"Mom, when church makes you feel so good, why don't you go more often?

John answered him,

"Because she wants us to go with her and we won't do that."

When Marc died, one of my concerns was where to hold the memorial service. Since Marc had struggled against church during his life, it didn't seem right to take him there in his death.

We held the memorial service in the funeral home.

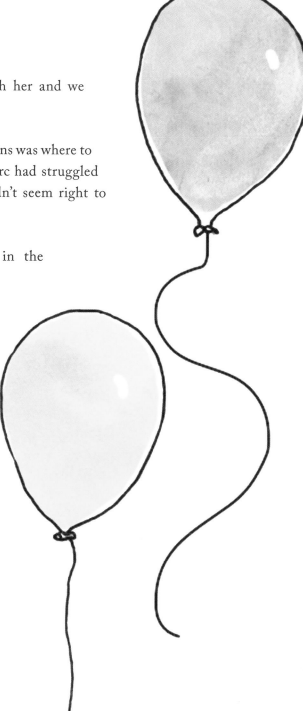

It's cold in our house and in the world. From my chair by the oven, I see the Christmas candle still burning, a dancing yellow flame of hope. Beyond the flame a green philodendron flourishes near the window. Outside the window, snow is dragging down the branches of a pine tree.

What is it I want to write about? Today I'll write about joy. Strange to feel such joy at a funeral!

Marilyn McDonald helped us plan the service. Marilyn and I had worked together at Emmaus, Services for the Aging, in Washington, D.C. We'd often walked the inner city streets together, going to visit clients. Our conversation on those long walks forged a deep friendship.

Now my family needed help. A traditional funeral didn't seem to fit Marc. Above all, it must be honest, true to the person of Marc.

We decided that each of us would write a letter to Marc to be read during the service. Marilyn suggested three readings from *The Prophet* by Kahlil Gibran, "On Children," "On Friendship," and "On Death." We would allow time for friends to speak.

This became the framework for the service.

On Children

And a woman who held a babe against her bosom said,

Speak to us of Children.

And he said:

Your children are not your children.

They are the sons and daughters of Life's longing for itself.

They come through you but not from you,

And though they are with you, yet they belong not to you.

You may give them your love but not your thoughts.

For they have their own thoughts.

You may house their bodies but not their souls,

For their souls dwell in the house of tomorrow,

which you cannot visit, not even in your dreams.

You may strive to be like them,

but seek not to make them like you.

For life goes not backward nor tarries with yesterday.

You are the bows from which your children

as living arrows are sent forth.

The archer sees the mark upon the path of the infinite,

and He bends you with His might

that His arrows may go swift and far.

Let your bending in the archer's hand be for gladness;

For even as He loves the arrow that flies,

so He loves also the bow that is stable.

from *The Prophet* by Kahlil Gibran

January 7, 1986

We wrote our letters.

They were not profound,
but writing them eased our need to talk with Marc.

I was afraid
I wouldn't be able to read my letter in the service,
but my voice held strong and clear.

It wobbled only at the end.

Dear Marc,

Your going is so painful. It is only bearable in that it seems you must know how deeply we love you.

Always I loved you, Marc. It seemed you were moving down a road so intently, and I was moving down another. Sometimes our roads ran together, and that was a gift from God!

It's hard to express this, Marc, but I'm proud that you were able to do things that were important to you. You made us understand, even about the motorcycle.

When you swung your bike around and up the hill, I often felt a surge of joy because you rode so well. I knew that mattered to you. Your coordination was a gift I learned to appreciate.

Lots of times you were a tarnation, a baffling predicament to me, but my world is bigger because of you. I know I'm wiser because you were there, pushing the boundaries.

You were a high-spirited burst of energy through almost nineteen years of my life. I'll study the rest of my life, hoping to understand all you have meant to me.

Godspeed, Marc!

Love, Mom

January 8, 1986

When John read his letter, I was distracted by his appearance.

He was just starting to let his beard grow again,
and the new growth looked unkempt.

Would people understand?

He was neither clean-shaven nor bearded.

I couldn't pay attention to what he was reading.

Dear Marc,

Writing this isn't easy. Not because I can't think of things to say. Rather, there are too many thoughts and feelings I want to express. I'm sad that I didn't say them sooner.

I hope you realize, Marc, that I love you. I have always loved you and will continue to love you, my Marc.

I regret there were too few occasions when you were able to talk to me about your feelings. However, one time you did. You tearfully told me that no one liked you, that you had no friends, that there must be something wrong with you. Marc, you have many, many friends—young, old, white, black, male, female—who honestly love you and have said that you're a great guy. There is nothing wrong with you.

Marc, I have learned from you the importance of forging ahead on your own road, of being yourself. You have taught me that not everyone has to live life by my values. I have learned from you the joy of exuberance, the pride of a job well done. You have taught me the importance of letting people know I love them, and letting them know now. Tomorrow may be too late!

Marc, I am a richer person because of you. Sharing your life has been a great happiness for me. Because of you I will be better able to say, "I love." Thank you, Marc. I'll miss you. But as you said to me Thursday morning, when you left for work,

"I'll see ya later."

Love, Dad

On Friendship

And a youth said, Speak to us of Friendship.

And he answered, saying:

Your friend is your needs answered.

He is your field which you sow with

love and reap with thanksgiving.

And he is your board and your fireside.

For you come to him with your hunger,

and you seek him for peace.

When your friend speaks his mind you fear not the

"nay" in your own mind, nor do you withhold the "ay."

And when he is silent your heart ceases

not to listen to his heart;

For without words, in friendship, all thoughts,

all desires, all expectations are born and

shared, with joy that is unacclaimed.

When you part from your friend, you grieve not;

For that which you love most in him may be

clearer in his absence, as the mountain to

the climber is clearer from the plain.

And let there be no purpose in friendship

save the deepening of the spirit.

For love that seeks aught but the disclosure

of its own mystery is not love but a net cast

forth: and only the unprofitable is caught.

And let your best be for your friend.

If he must know the ebb of your tide,

let him know its flood also.

For what is your friend that you should

seek him with hours to kill?

Seek him always with hours to live.

For it is his to fill your need, but not your emptiness.

And in the sweetness of friendship let there

be laughter, and sharing of pleasures.

For in the dew of little things the heart

finds its morning and is refreshed.

from *The Prophet* by Kahlil Gibran

January 9, 1986

Carole read her letter
after the Gibran reading, "On Friendship."

I was startled when, instead of walking to the podium,
she went around and in back of the coffin,
working her way through the flower arrangements
to the head of the coffin.

She told me later that she was trying
to get as close to Marc as possible.

Fortunately, none of the flower stands fell over.

We were all a little crazy in our intensity.

Dear Marc,

We have walked together down a wooded path.

With each curve in the trail, each tree and rock, we have grown. Sometimes things along the way would make you react differently than me, but that was okay.

Now that you have chosen a different path to walk on, I feel so lost and alone.

My dear, sweet brother, I just want you to know that I love you.

Wherever our different paths lead us, we will always be together.

Love, Carole

The crowd.

We never expected such a large gathering. The funeral home director asked how many we expected, and I thought it would be a small group.

Oh, the crowd that gathered!

Neighbors, old and young
Marc's school friends
men from Acme Iron Works
friends of Carole's from school and work
colleagues of John's
teachers from Harmony Hall
friends from Foundry Church.

I thought surely they had forgotten us, but here they were, friends and friends and friends.

We were surrounded by love.

Mike was beautiful! He was the boy who slept overnight at our house and wrestled on the lawn with Carole—according to the indignant talk of the neighbors.

I found his first love letters around our house, and I swept around his electric trains on the floor of Marc's room. I knew the neighbor kid, Mike, but not the man standing in front of the crowd.

When had his shoulders and chest begun to fill out his jacket? Where had he learned to project his voice? I felt so proud of him!

Mike began,

"I've been trying to remember when Marc first came into my life. It seems like he's always been there."

I can tell you, Mike. We moved to Fairhill Drive just after Marc's fourth birthday. Carole was six. Before the moving truck was unloaded, Mike and his brother, Vaughn, had scrambled up the embankment to tell them,

"Hi! There's no Santa Claus."

Mike must have been eight and Vaughn nine when they blew away our Christmas illusions.

How many times in the years to come did I answer the front door to find Mike, too shy to look at me, asking for Marc through a chin locked to his chest?

Now here he was, speaking in a voice that resonated through the crowd.

"Marc and I had many good talks. One question concerned him:

"'How do you tell your parents you love them?'"

"So often in conversation, Marc would struggle with that problem,

"'How do you tell your parents you love them?'"

Holding me securely with his eyes, Mike said,

"Marc loved you very much."

Carole's friend, David, spoke to the crowd, but his remarks were for her.

"I remember when we came to your house last Christmas. You were introducing your family to us, when you said,

"'And this is my handsome brother, Marc!'"

"I looked at Marc to see how he would react. Most kid brothers would bristle self-consciously, but Marc looked at you with a smile. It was a look of love, Carole."

I had noticed that look, too. Lively affection and an irrepressible smile had played across Marc's face.

Though often silent and gruff, Marc had that look sometimes.

I had forgotten until David reminded me: Marc had that look of love.

Our old neighbors, John, Penny and Mark Sylvester, flew up from Florida to attend the funeral. Mark Sylvester was one of Marc's best friends. His dad said,

"Of all the friends of our children who have come through our home, Marc Mathews was undoubtedly the favorite."

Mark Sylvester. We always called him by his full name to distinguish him from our own Marc.

Once when they were pre-schoolers, I was playing "lions and tigers" with them. Amidst growls and scampering around on the floor, I suddenly felt teeth in my shoulder. One little tiger had crossed over the line of imagination and was defending himself against my ferocious roar.

I gripped my shoulder, held the child, and exclaimed,

"Mark Sylvester! Don't ever do that! That hurts!"

I never heard of him biting anyone again. Maybe grown-up tears did the job.

Mark Sylvester's birthday was July 9, 1963, and that gave him ten glorious days each year when he and Marc Mathews were the same age. A four-year-old Mark Sylvester came to Marc's fifth birthday party in a white shirt and short pants. He was expecting to be the only guest, but at the last minute other neighbor children came, too. I can still see Penny sitting on the stone steps with her little boy, trying to help him make sense of other guests at a party.

Marc Mathews was killed on his friend's birthday, July 9, and Mark Sylvester was one of the pallbearers.

My close friend, Janice McMurray, spoke at the funeral. She and her friends had been camping deep in the mountains of North Carolina when her daughter, Nissen, reached them with the news. Janice called me immediately to say she would come.

Her comments surprised me.

At the time I was enmeshed in my failure. To have my child's life crushed out seemed the ultimate failure for me as a parent. Janice said,

"What a privilege to have grown up in this family! Camping trips in the mountains, children's choirs, plays, Christmas in Texas, all the wonderful experiences you have shared as a family!"

Her comments helped to lift my spirits. There were some things we had done right. It helped to be reminded of that.

Nancy Myers stood up to speak at the funeral, but her sobs broke off her words.

Nancy had three children: Matt, Laura and Glenda. Marc spent a lot of time at their house. I think, actually, he wanted to be part of their family. Nancy told me Marc often left after she had gone to bed.

"He would be revving up his motorcycle, and I'd lie there after a long day at the hospital, wondering if he'd ever get out of there with that awful noise. Now I'd gladly listen to his motorcycle for hours."

Matt was a reedy, shy, young man. He'd knock on our front door and then study something out on the street when I answered. One day I opened the door to a really scrumptious young man in a navy uniform. The fit of that uniform was perfection! So was Matt.

Recently we met Matt's new baby, a little bald newborn. His name is Wesley, Marc's middle name.

"Marc was the only Wesley I ever knew," Matt said.

Matt's sister, Laura, is a lovely girl. Nancy told me that Laura and Marc were boyfriend and girlfriend for a while.

I visited Marc's grave on his birthday, just 10 days after he died. A large sheaf of roses covered the grave, with a note tucked in.

I hesitated, wondering if it would be rude of me to read the note, but I wanted to know who had left him flowers. I slipped off the ribbon and unrolled the piece of paper.

> I give you nineteen roses for nineteen years of life. Six are yellow for the six years you brightened my life. You will always live on in my memories.
>
> With Love
> Laura

I still have that note. I read it from time to time. It helps to know that Marc was loved.

We ended the service by reading from Gibran, "On Death."

On Death

Then Almitra spoke, saying, We would ask now of Death.

And he said:

You would know the secret of death.

But how shall you find it unless you

seek it in the heart of life?

The owl whose night-bound eyes are blind unto

the day cannot unveil the mystery of light.

If you would indeed behold the spirit of death,

open your heart wide unto the body of life.

For life and death are one, even as

the river and the sea are one.

In the depth of your hopes and desires lies

your silent knowledge of the beyond;

And like seeds dreaming beneath the

snow your heart dreams of spring.

Trust the dreams, for in them is hidden the gate to eternity.

Your fear of death is but the trembling

of the shepherd when

he stands before the king whose hand is

to be laid upon him in honour.

Is the shepherd not joyful beneath his trembling,

that he shall wear the mark of the king?

Yet is he not more mindful of his trembling?

For what is it to die but to stand naked in

the wind and to melt into the sun?

And what is it to cease breathing, but to free

the breath from its restless tides, that it may rise

and expand and seek God unencumbered?

Only when you drink from the river of

silence shall you indeed sing.

And when you have reached the mountain

top, then you shall begin to climb.

And when the earth shall claim your

limbs, then shall you truly dance.

from *The Prophet* by Kahlil Gibran

Something ending.
Something beginning.

The Easter after Marc died, John, Carole Jo and I went to Foundry Church together.

As we entered the sanctuary, we were caught up in a celebration of color: white lilies, red and pink azaleas, balloons of every color!

Balloons everywhere!

Balloons escaped, up and up, trapped and bouncing against the high dome in the ceiling. Every once in a while, another balloon broke loose and gently floated to the heights.

And, of course, an occasional balloon burst, here and there. During the sermon Dr. Bauman would pause to acknowledge the disruptive popping with a grin.

I felt myself drawn into what he was saying, but kept holding back.

I knew that if I could accept the Easter message, so many things would make sense.

Was it just that I wanted to believe? Surely life would be better if I could believe.

All these years I'd held my doubts before me like a shield. I didn't want to be a gullible fool, but I hadn't gotten anywhere my way, either.

In my reverie I dreamily became aware of a stray balloon, drifting over our heads from the back of the church toward the front. Anyone could reach up to stop its meandering journey, but no one did.

I totally lost track of the sermon as I watched the balloon tilt off to the left, seemingly headed for Dr. Bauman's face.

Then it paused, floated to the right and around in back of the pulpit, over the heads of the choir, and on to the altar.

I lost track of the balloon as a sudden realization hit me: That's a blue balloon!

It's Marc's favorite color!

It's almost as though Marc is talking to me.

"You can accept what he's saying, Mom. There is resurrection and life! You can go with it. It's okay. Let yourself accept."

Last night I asked Carole to tell me about the brake drum again. Either I didn't listen carefully the first time, or I had forgotten.

Years later, I was ready to hear the story.

Several months after Marc died, Carole was visiting her friend, Jim, who had an old Volvo sports car. For several weekends he had been trying to remove a frozen brake drum from the car.

Special tools had been rented and broken, friends had tried unsuccessfully to help.

Saturday morning Jim was struggling once again to remove the brake drum.

Another tool broke.

He threw it down on the pavement in exasperation and stormed into his apartment, slamming the door behind him.

Carole knelt on the pavement to look closely at the brake drum, thinking that perhaps a novice might bring fresh insight to the situation.

Then she thought of her brother.

"Marc, I need your help."

Carole placed her hands on either side of the brake drum and simply lifted it out. She ran into Jim's apartment.

"The brake drum is out."

"Sure, Carole. That's very funny."

"No, really, it's out. It's lying in the parking lot."

"That's impossible!"

"Well, come out and see."

Jim stared in disbelief at the brake drum lying on the pavement near the car. Carole chuckled and thought,

"Thank you, Marc!"

On the first anniversary of Marc's death, July 9, 1982, John and I met Carole Jo in College Park for dinner. John told us a new mockingbird story.

Thursday, the day before the anniversary, John had been working on a furniture refinishing project in the back yard.

His table was set up out on the brick patio, loaded down with tools, newspapers and rags. Old paint from the chair he was stripping, mixed with paint stripper, was smeared all over the table.

Sadness and despair were dragging John into hopelessness, but he kept going through the motions of working. A mockingbird flew onto the table, perched there amidst the noxious mess for a few moments, then flew away.

"John, you're kidding!"

"No, it happened! I was stripping old paint from a chair, feeling very sad, when a bird flew down onto the table, a mockingbird."

"Why didn't you tell me yesterday?"

"I wanted to wait until we were all together to tell it."

"But today is the anniversary."

"Yesterday was Thursday. Marc was killed on a Thursday. Yesterday was the hardest day for me."

February 23, 1986

A grandchild has been born, a round-faced girl with red hair and blue eyes.

Emma Elizabeth Dennis.

"Surprised by joy"—that phrase describes perfectly how it feels to have your first grandchild.

Carole visited last Monday with Emma. She asked me,

"Mom, are you still seeing mockingbirds everywhere? This morning I dressed Emma and laid her on the bed while I got dressed myself. When I turned back, there was a mockingbird on the windowsill, looking in through the glass at Emma."

I sat with Lucy Tang for a couple hours today.

Lucy, a longtime member of Foundry Church, is in the final stages of terminal cancer. She wants to live her last weeks in her own apartment, so several of us from the church are taking turns sitting with her.

Lucy is very weak now, her body little more than a rack on which to hang the cancer, but today she asked me to help her walk.

She was insistent, so we struggled to get her on her feet. She surprised me by walking completely around her apartment a couple times.

What determination in taking those steps!

For just a few minutes she had control over her life. It was hard to get her back onto the bed, and I'm sure the clumsy struggle hurt her.

She lay against the pillow, exhausted.

She called me "an angel from God."

After my time with Lucy, I stepped out into a cold, rainy day. I was thinking that Lucy is just 50 years old, my age exactly.

What a contrast—her painful prison and my walk in the rain! I gave thanks for the gift of life and health. I felt renewed hope that I might live my life well.

Just then a mockingbird flew directly in front of me and settled on the brick wall nearby. I stood quietly watching him.

He stayed there a few minutes, then flew away. Yet another affirmation for me: I am alive and healthy. My life is a gift and I am grateful.

I will celebrate my life!

On the way home, for good measure, I followed a white truck with a big red cardinal painted on the back.

I had to laugh.

Can I overlook these tokens?

Why throw them away?

Joy!

I'm thinking today of another token I was given three years ago. Someone had told me,

"You will see Marc.
It will be perfectly natural.
You will see his face superimposed on someone else's face,
and this will be his way of saying, Hi!"

On a winter's day I was driving to an appointment in Virginia. As I came off the freeway exit, I had to immediately cross two lanes of traffic for a left-hand turn. The left-hand lane was backed up, so I pulled my car into the adjoining lane.

As the light changed, a young man in the truck alongside me leaned over and gestured for me to pull in ahead of him.

It was Marc!

In a rush of recognition, I waved and smiled. As I pulled into his lane, I realized he was driving a blue truck.

The light turned green and we made our turns, the blue truck right behind me.

As we drove down the road, I kept looking in my rear view mirror at a silhouette of Marc: the erect way of holding his body, his size, the unruly blond hair sticking out, even the angle of the cap.

It was Marc.

He followed me for a mile or two until I made my left turn into the shopping center.

"So long, Marc. Thanks for showing up."

I had to go into the shop and pretend to be a normal, reasonable person. I did that, but later, on the way home, I started to cry.

The days that followed were filled with tension, chaos and emotional turmoil, but I kept seeing the kid in a blue truck on the road behind me.

"It's okay, Mom. You're not in this alone."

Yesterday after the church service I went into Fellowship Hall for the coffee hour. A chance conversation at the punch bowl reminded me of a happy memory: the Children's Choir singing "Lord of the Dance."

> Dance, then, wherever you may be.
>
> I am the Lord of the Dance, said He.
>
> And I'll lead you all wherever you may be,
>
> And I'll lead you all in the dance, said He.

In their early grade school years, Carole Jo and Marc were both in the Children's Choir at Foundry Church. I was rehearsing the children as Dr. Bauman, our senior minister, sat on the floor, leaning against a choir pew.

"You know, this is so joyful! It's a shame for the children to just stand there. Could they move in some way to match their singing?"

"Okay! We'll dance around the church!" With a child's hand in each of mine, left and right, I called out to the rest,

"Come on, everybody, let's go!"

The children came scrambling down the steps, skipping, whirling, running, laughing and singing up the center aisle. Some went this way, some that, down the sides and back to the center, up the steps to the altar, all out of breath and full of excitement.

Oh, the cheeks and eyes!
The wonderful faces!

But even through their breathless laughter I could see fear and misgivings as they looked to me for direction, wondering if they could really do this happy, outrageous thing in the middle of Sunday worship.

What would their parents think? I wondered the same thing myself.

People filled the sanctuary the following Sunday. The Children's Choir followed the Cathedral Choir in a formal procession to the altar. Starched white smocks over royal blue cassocks disguised our excitement. The children took their places on the altar steps.

When our turn came to sing, no one held back. Holding hands, skipping, turning, running, flying, we danced all over the church.

We became the Lord of the Dance. No, Christ was Lord of the Dance.

The children were the dance.

When we came back to the altar, and before the song was quite finished, the congregation burst into applause even more exuberant than our dance!

"Lord of the Dance" uses the Shaker Hymn tune, "Simple Gifts," my first choice of songs for Marc's memorial service.

Simple Gifts

'Tis the gift to be simple, 'Tis the gift to be free.

'Tis the gift to come down where we ought to be.

And when we find ourselves in the place just right,

'Twill be in the valley of love and delight.

I'm thinking again of the blue balloon that caught my attention that Easter Sunday after Marc's death.

A balloon is not a religious thing,
not sacred, not profound or wise,
just a playful and fragile invention of this world.

On that Easter Sunday, however, the balloon became for me a sign, telling me I can believe in a God who loves me.

A loving God gave us a son to teach us there is no death. And because the balloon was blue, my son's favorite color, I believe my own son is part of the mystery.

I have tumbled this way and that with my questions and doubts.

God guided a blue balloon down through the congregation toward a minister speaking words of hope.

I started, in that moment, to accept my own belief.

For the last year I've been working for a spiritualist minister, Anne Gehman, doing general office things, appointments, bills, correspondence. Sometime in late September I asked Anne to work with me for fifteen minutes. Since Marc's death I'd had so many physical problems. With all the medical attention, my body still hurt. Anne's gift of spiritual healing might help.

As Anne meditated, she said,

"Sally, a young man is here. I think he's your son. Was your son's name Marc?"

"Yes."

"He's showing me a rainbow. Do you know what it means? He's asking you to forgive him. What do you need to forgive? Why would he ask you to forgive him?"

That evening I related the story to John. Why would I need to forgive Marc? At first it seemed a general thing. Marc and I had struggled together. Maybe he's sorry he made it so hard on me in his growing up.

In the car, John asked me again,

"Is there something Marc did you need to forgive?"

My growled curse caught me by surprise,

"Yes! He promised me he would not get killed on that motorcycle!"

The harsh shout, the sobs, the violence of old pain crashed around in our car. How long had it been?

Six years.

It had been six years since the accident,
and now this bitter accusation,
a promise broken!

Shaking with tears and stunned into silence, we drove home. I was exhausted. My heart felt smashed open by unexpected anger.

I hadn't known the pain was there!

Gradually, healing began. The words were not spoken out loud, but I'm sure he heard them,

"I forgive you, Marc."

I went to bed and slept a long, deep sleep.

Weeping may endure for a night,
but joy cometh in the morning.

Psalms 30:5

I'm remembering again.

I am at Kirkridge Retreat Center in October of 1987. I've just taken a long walk on the Appalachian Trail with a new friend. It's a beautiful fall day, the air brisk, the sky a wonder of blue, colors of the trees, spectacular!

I cannot sit still for the Bible study, so I decide to visit the little stone chapel I've heard about.

A steep mountain trail leads me through woods to a round stone structure in a garden of great rocks. I slide the bolt in a heavy wooden door and find myself in a miniature church.

It's hardly more than a round room with leaded glass windows, the roof pointing up into a spire of timbers and glass, open to blue sky and dazzling sunlight.

I am dancing, laughing, praying, singing, shouting.

Shouting!

I have learned to shout at God this week.

"God! I want you to listen to me!
Do you hear me, God?
Listen and hear me!"

I sit on the wooden pew and try to meditate, but I can't contain the energy coursing through me. I kneel on the floor with my face against the cold stones.

What is my prayer?

What words will say it for me?

104

I jump up again and leap about on the stones, and then I am shouting to the heavens, singing,

> Dance, then, wherever you may be.
>
> I am the Lord of the Dance, said He.
>
> And I'll lead you all, wherever you may be.
>
> And I'll lead you all in the dance, said He.

It's the Shaker tune again, and Marc is singing with me.

Everyone I ever loved is with me, and we are all dancing together through death into life.

This is joy!

Joy that reaches into heaven where my heart has searched and joy that makes of earth open arms for heaven. All of life and all the world are in my song. Here in a tiny stone chapel I embrace life.

I circle the great stone in the center and join a chorus of people who have ever felt pain and waited.

Surely the joy does come!

This week marks the seventh anniversary of Marc's death. I know that as a fact.

I also know that I'm feeling sad, yet I can't seem to make the connection. The cause of my sadness is not clear to me.

We went to visit Carole and Tim at the ocean last month. It was fun watching Emma play on the beach.

It's so easy to delight in her!

John and I walked on the beach Thursday, catching the shimmer of early morning sunlight on the water.

"Send a prayer out over the water."

Where did I first hear that? It's a good thought.

Of course, John, Carole, Tim and Emma slip into my prayers first, but that morning on the beach I felt close to Marc, and I said my old, old prayer for him:

"Dear God, be with Marc. Wherever he may be, I pray that he may be with you. Let Marc know that I love him. Lord, let Marc know that he is loved!"

Some pictures of Marc fishing at the beach came to mind. Carole framed a series of three shots that are hanging on the wall in Marc's old room.

Navy swim trunks reveal long skinny legs and the inevitable baseball cap barely holds the unruly blond hair.

The gray ocean is rolling in with some white froth and seems to go on forever.

In the first shot Marc has his back to the camera. His left foot is grounded in the sand, but his right foot is lifting into the movement of casting his line out over the water.

The effort of casting a line brings his muscles into play, and we see them clearly in the thin arms, the arching back and the taut legs.

In the next picture Marc is looking back at us through silvered sunglasses. A trace of fuzzy down is there over a lip that's curled up in a "what're ya doin'?" expression.

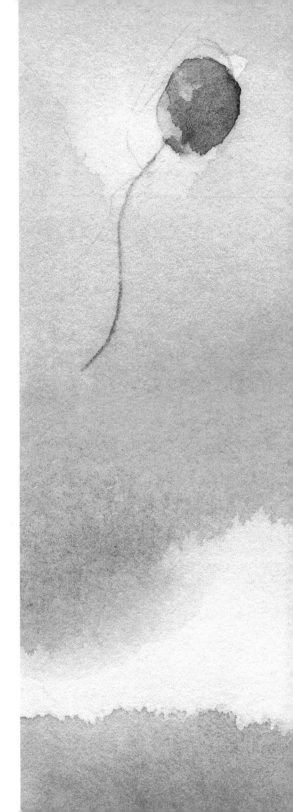

In the last picture, Marc is standing sideways, holding his rod with a fish dangling from the line. He looks at us just over the sunglasses, and his expression says both,

"Look what I've done!" and "What're you lookin' at?"

As we walked along, I imagined other pictures of Marc, looking out over the ocean, different sizes of the same boy. I couldn't help thinking,

"How I long to know that Marc is with us, here where he liked to be."

It was a great walk, almost an hour and a half. Hardly anyone was out on the beach so early. I walked barefoot, digging my toes into the sand.

I was looking down at my feet, careful not to step on anything sharp, when John said,

"There's your blue balloon."

I looked up to see a blue balloon floating by in the water, watched it go past me, turned around several times to look again, and finally thought,

"Hey, this is kind of unusual. I ought to get it."

By now the waves had carried the balloon away from me. I had to scurry and splash about to catch it.

"John, how did you happen to see the balloon? I never would have seen it if you hadn't said something."

"Oh, I've been watching it for a while. At first it was way out there. Then it was carried in toward the shore. That woman has been trying to catch it, but every time she almost had it, a wave washed it back out again."

"You saw it from way out there? Why didn't you tell me about it?"

"I wasn't really thinking about it being a blue balloon until it floated right beside you. Then I realized, 'That's Sally's blue balloon.'"

The other woman smiled as I passed her with the balloon in my hand. I wanted to tell her why the balloon had gotten away from her over and over again and then just came to me.

When we walked into the apartment, Emma grabbed the balloon and started to play with it. Carole smiled,

"Where did you get that?"

"It was in the water."

"That balloon was in the ocean?"

"Yep. It washed in on a wave right up to me."

"Emma, give it back. That's Grandma's balloon."

That's when it finally occurred to me.

I had longed for a tangible sign that Marc was walking with us.

To think that I almost didn't reach out when it came to me.

*To every thing there is a season, and a
time to every purpose under the heaven:
a time to be born, and a time to die.*

Ecclesiastes 3:1-2

I've been working at Carole's house today. Emma came in from school and immediately put her favorite song on the stereo to dance. The song is called "One More Time," and she has continued to play it one more time throughout the afternoon.

She climbed into the chair beside the computer, wanting to be part of my project.

"Are there bad things in the story?"

"What do you mean, Emma?"

"Does someone die?"

"Yes, Emma. You know your Mommy had a brother who died. I've been writing about that." Emma thought for a moment, then asked,

"Is there laughter in the story?"

"Yes, some laughter."

"Why?"

"Well, it's a little hard to explain. It's not really funny, but now that it's all written down, there may be more laughter. It's like when you come home from school, you put on the music and dance.

Well, I've been working on this for a long time, sort of like going to school. Now I'd like to try more dancing."

A time to weep, and a time to laugh;
a time to mourn, and a time to dance.

Ecclesiastes 3:4

EPILOGUE

September 18, 2013

Sixteen years have passed, again! It's been sixteen years since I wrote the Prologue, sixteen years since I've seriously engaged with this work. There have been some grand adventures, so I'll mention a few.

John and I ventured to Ireland for six months. We immersed ourselves in the paradoxical spirit of that beautiful green land, home of my ancestors. We walked and walked and walked. When we could not walk somewhere, we journeyed by bus, train, bicycle and mule-drawn cart. Also, occasionally, car. Ireland's treasures — centuries-old high crosses, monastic ruins, ancient Celtic sites, windy seacoast — all of them seemed to weave a mystical charm around us.

When we returned to the United States, we no longer fit our lives. Kirkridge Retreat Center lured us to the Kittatinny Mountains of Pennsylvania, idyllic setting for thought-provoking retreats. We served as Kirkridge staff associates for three years, but we still had not come home.

A retreatant invited us to her picturesque town on the Susquehanna River, and we liked it so much we stayed. At home in Lewisburg we've joined an elite group, the elderly.

We're great-grandparents. Yes! Emma has her own little round-faced baby. We call him "Jack." My sweetest joy is knowing Carole and Tim's delight in their grandchild.

Our thoughts never wander far from Marc.

He's still part of our lives.

    Sadness moves in, sometimes, but mostly we live with gratitude for our son and the world he opened for us. Coping with Marc's death has been a lifetime task. Even so, it's a good life.

MARC WESLEY MATHEWS
1962-1981

ACKNOWLEDGEMENTS

September 18, 2013

Thanking folks who helped with *The Blue Balloon* would mean naming everybody who has been part of my life. I cannot name them all!

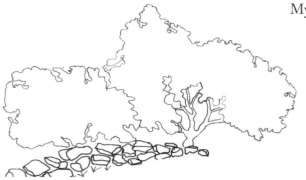

My deepest gratitude to John, life partner for more than fifty years. Humor and imagination have brought life to the journey we travel together. Thank you for making the book possible.

Our daughter, Carole Jo, provided pen and ink drawings for the book. Thank you, Carole, for so many things, but especially your gifts of drawing.

Kathryn Schifferdecker, thank you for your youthful generosity. You sorted through a grocery bag of my journal pages and helped me shape a book. Marjory Bankson read that first manuscript and telephoned me, offering encouragement.

Janice McMurray became a friend when Marc was a few months old. When I requested something for the book cover, she sent several possibilities. We used them all. Thank you, Janice, for the watercolors.

Dorothy Baumwoll has nudged many of us with pen and paper. In her classes I slowly began to understand that I needed to complete my work with this manuscript. Thank you, Dot, for your writing workshops.

Prudence McCullough helped me get *The Blue Balloon* out of a box in the attic and into working shape on our computers. Thank you, Prudence, for your copyediting.

Cindy Peltier magically connected me with Elise Nicol, book designer. Finally, all things have come together! Thank you, Elise. My book waited for you, all these years.

Dear family, friends, teachers, and helpers, I'm grateful you've been part of my life.

Thank you.